Grand Teton National Park

Attractions & Sights to See

Billy Grinslott & Kinsey Marie Books

ISBN - 9781965098004

The Teton Park Road runs along the base of the Teton Mountain Range, connecting Moose and Jackson Lake Junction. Along the road are multiple pull-offs and overlooks. Trailheads such as Taggart Lake, Lupine Meadows, Jenny Lake, String and Leigh Lakes, and Signal Mountain can be accessed from the Teton Park Road.

The Jenny Lake Loop travels along the edge of Jenny Lake, providing hikers with stunning views. This loop trail provides a variety of views including Cascade Canyon, the Cathedral Group, and Jenny Lake. The Jenny Lake Loop is a 7.1-mile hike with 1,040 feet of elevation gain. Generally considered a moderately challenging hike. This Trail loops around Jenny lake and offers beautiful views.

Schwabacher Landing. Discover this 0.5-mile out-and-back trail near Moose, Wyoming. Generally considered an easy route. Schwabacher Landing is located along Snake River. It is a short walk from the parking area with a view of the Tetons. The road is off U.S. Highway 191. Look for beavers in this area, they have built many beaver dams in the area, creating ponds.

The 42-mile Grand Teton Scenic Drive loop is a stress-free way to see Grand Teton National Park. Driving this loop offers stunning views of the Teton Range, along with the opportunity to view wildlife. Many turnouts along park roads offer exhibits on park information, wildlife, and plants. The Turnouts provide safe places to enjoy scenic views of the park, views of wildlife, and the opportunity to take photographs.

Jackson Lake is a huge lake in Grand Teton National Park with stunning views of the surrounding mountains. You can easily drive to spots that offer picnic areas, the Jackson Lake overlook or visit the Jackson Lake dam. Another great way to see Jackson Lake is to take a boat tour. This 15-mile-long glacial lake is located at the base of the Tetons mountains. It has become a recreational destination, with visitors flocking to its shores for fishing, boating and camping.

The Cascade Canyon Trail will bring you deep into Grand Teton National Park. Cascade Canyon Trail offers incredible views, wildlife sightings, and beautiful scenery. Hikers are met with stunning views of the surrounding mountains while hiking through Cascade Canyon. Amazing hike from start to end. The hike is only hard because it is 9.3 miles round trip.

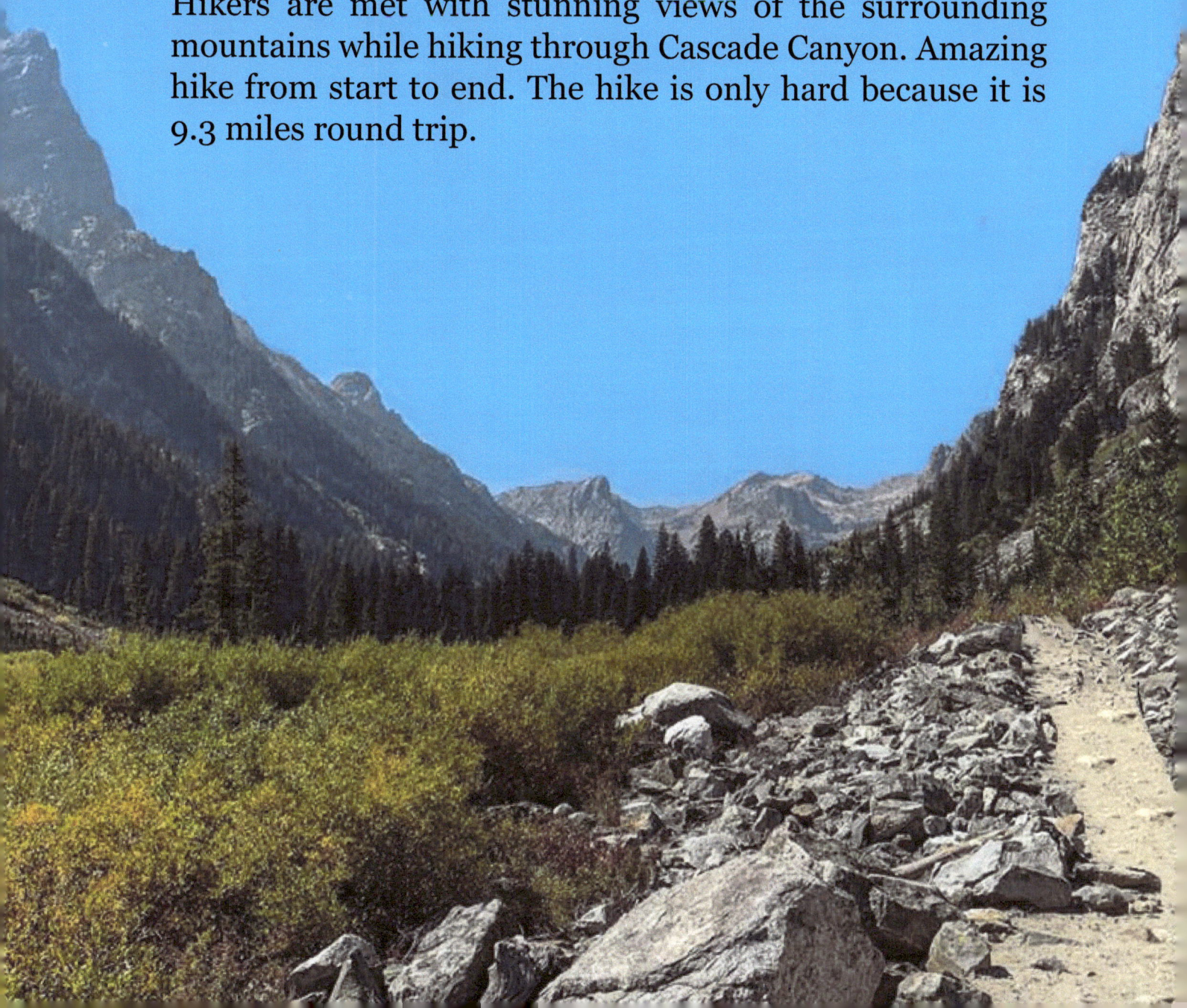

Signal Mountain is 7,727 feet high it is in Jackson Hole. Visitors can access the summit by car or foot. From the summit, visitors have panoramic views of Jackson Hole and the Teton Range. The Signal Mountain hiking trail winds up a forested mountainside to the summit. The trail is a moderate, 6.8 miles out and back trail. For easier access to the summit, drive the Teton Park Road and Turn left onto Signal Mountain Summit Road.

Taggart Lake is an easy, out and back 3.3-mile roundtrip trail that offers visitors some of the best views of the Teton Range. Hikers will wind up an aspen-covered moraine before the trail opens up to views of the Tetons. The trail then flattens out and heads to the lakeshore. Hikers will find spectacular views of an alpine lake with the Teton Range behind it. This trail is a perfect hike to do with the family as it doesn't gain very much elevation and it has stunning views year-round

Inspiration Point is one of the most popular trails within the park. Hiking to Hidden Falls and Inspiration Point has spectacular views of Jenny Lake, a 100 ft cascading waterfall, and the Jackson Hole Valley. You can also enjoy views of Cascade Canyon, the Cathedral Group, Mount Owen, TeeWinot, and the Grand Tetons. Visitors may choose to walk around the southern lakeshore or utilize the privately-run shuttle boat to cross the lake and shorten the hike. Inspiration Point is an easy, 1.8 mile out and back hike

The Rockefeller Preserve is a 1,106-acre refuge within Grand Teton National Park on the southern end of Phelps Lake. The Preserve features several sightseeing opportunities and a variety of wildflowers and animal species. You can drive right to the preserve and then hike the Rockefeller Preserve Trailhead 3 miles roundtrip. Or you can hike the 6.4-mile roundtrip Phelps Lake Loop Trail. They also have a visitor center there.

No roads go to Leigh Lake, it is only accessible by foot or by boat. You can access it by portaging from string lake or by hiking to it via the Leigh Lake 3-mile loop trail. At the halfway point of the trail, you will reach one of the most scenic spots along the shore of Leigh Lake. Here you will have outstanding views of the Tetons, Teewinot Mountain, Rockchuck Peak, Mt. Woodring and Mt. Moran.

Cascade Canyon is situated between Grand Teton which is 13,770 feet high to the south and several other peaks over 11,000 feet high to the north. Steep cliffs descend from these peaks and ensure awesome views of the mountains. The canyon was formed by glaciers. The Cascade Canyon Trail follows the length of the canyon. It is one of the most picturesque hikes in Grand Teton National Park.

Hidden Falls is a 100 ft cascading waterfall. Hiking to Hidden Falls allows for spectacular views of Jenny Lake and Jackson Hole. Visitors may choose to walk around the southern lakeshore or utilize the privately-run shuttle boat to cross the lake and shorten the hike.

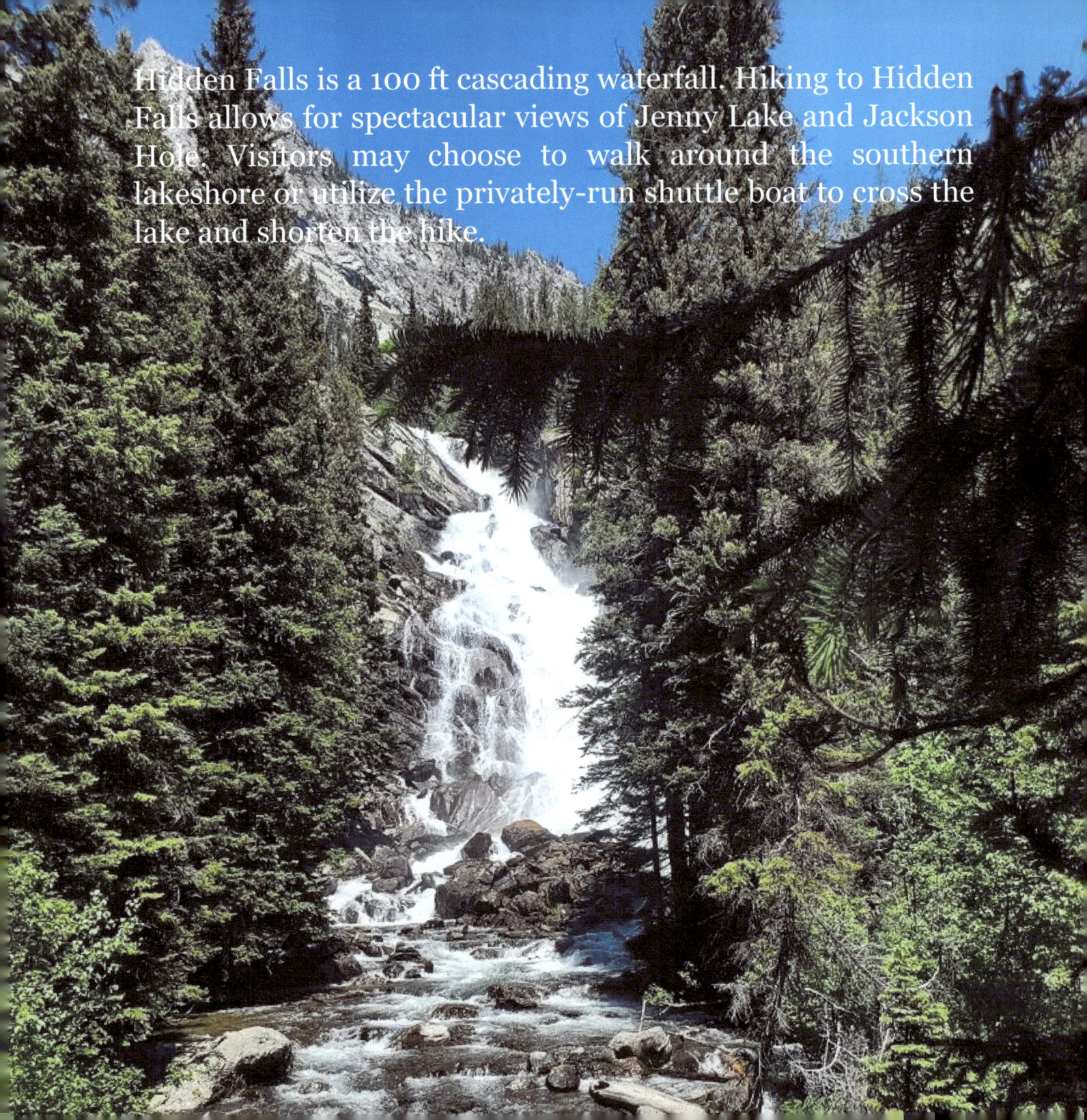

One of the most beautiful, side of the road, overlooks in Grand Teton National Park is the Snake River Overlook. It is one of the easiest overlooks to get to when traveling highway 191. You will have awesome views of the snake river and the Grand Teton Mountains in the background.

Lake Solitude gives you a view of the Grand Tetons in the background. This popular hike offers views of the surrounding peaks, alpine lakes, and ample wildlife viewing opportunities. This iconic National Park route is slotted in one of the most beautiful in the country. This 16.6-mile out-and-back trail is Generally considered a challenging route. But the views are well worth it.

Amphitheater Lake got its name because the mountains surround the lake kind of like you are sitting in an Amphitheater. It is an incredible hike to two subalpine lakes, with great views of Grand Tetons, Mt Owen, and Disappointment Peak. Explore this 9.9-mile out-and-back trail. Generally considered a challenging route.

The Moose Wilson Road is a connects the towns of Moose and Wilson. The road winds through forest and marsh habitats and is home to various species of wildlife. The road provides access to the Laurance S. Rockefeller Preserve, and the Granite and Death Canyon Trailheads. Moose Wilson Road is a narrow, mostly paved road. The Road is closed to RVs and trailers. The Moose Wilson Road is 7.1 miles-long

Teton Point Turnout is a turnout on the Grand Teton's 42 Mile loop drive. It is one that may surprise you with how much you can see and learn from here. This is a great turnout that has plenty of spaces for parking. You get some picture-perfect views of the Grand Tetons. This is one of several overlooks along Hwy 26 going north out of Grand Teton Park.

Jackson Lake Overlook is a great place to photograph the Tetons with the lake in the foreground. This is one of the best stops along the road to get a 360-degree photo of the Tetons. You can walk a bit and get varying vantage points. Jackson lake overlook is located off highway 191/89. There are plenty of pull-offs and places to stop for a picnic.

String Lake offers various opportunities for relaxation. String Lake is a popular area for picnics and swimming. Bring your own boat and paddle around. String Lake is a shallow lake and is warm making it a great place to swim. String Lake sits at the bottom of the Grand Teton Mountain range, and this trail provides visitors with stellar views of it. The trail loops around the Lake and is 3.7 mile trail that is fairly easy to walk.

The Death Canyon Trailhead offers access to Phelps Lake and into Death Canyon. Head out on this 25.5-mile loop trail near Moose, Wyoming. Generally considered a challenging route. There are other areas that to connect to it that are shorter routes. Some hikers make it a 2 day adventure while camping overnight. This beautiful hike up the canyon leads to wildflower meadows set beneath the mountains.

This hike to Grand Viewpoint begins from the Jackson Lake Lodge area. Discover this 5.0-mile roundtrip trail near Moran, Wyoming, considered a moderately challenging route. There is a shorter route available from the Grand Viewpoint Trailhead. Grand Viewpoint offers spectacular mountain and lake views. With panoramic views of the Teton Range and Jackson Hole.

Delta Lake Trail. Delta Lake is nestled right below Grand Teton, and it has the best up-close views of the mountains you can get. However, the 9-mile trail leading up to Delta Lake is unmaintained and requires a bit of navigation. The trail crosses boulder fields and ends with a steep climb. The turquoise-green color of the lake comes from the glacial silt fed by the Teton Glacier which you can see from the lake.

The Cathedral Group refers to three mountain peaks. Teewinot Mountain, the Grand Teton and Mount Owen. They appear as cathedral-like spires when viewed from the northeast along the Jenny Lake Scenic Loop Drive. The Cathedral Group Turnout captures both the beauty of the Teton Range and the surrounding landscape

The Targhee National Forest spans 3 million acres along the western borders of Yellowstone and Grand Teton National Park. It is accessible from West Yellowstone, Island Park, Teton Valley, Swan Valley, and Star Valley. This is an 8-mile, easy roundtrip hike. It's a beautiful trail that takes you through forest, valleys and meadows alongside Targhee Creek.

Glacier View Turnout is about 20 minutes north of Jackson, WY. On US-191 N/US-26/US-89. Glacier View Turnout provides a big picture view of three Teton glaciers. Middle, Teepee, and Teton on the Grand Teton range. There is plenty of parking and you don't have to enter the park for this stop. It is on the main highway. There is a display board with information related to this stop.

Hermitage point trail is 9.5 miles roundtrip leaving from the Colter Bay Marina parking lot. The Trail traverses rolling terrain through forests, meadows, and wetlands providing wildlife habitat views. Along the way you will see many of the park's mountains. The point overlooks an estuary of the creeks that run into Jackson Lake. You'll also be able to see the Jackson Lake Dam in the far-off distance.

Lakeshore Trail is an easy 2-mile loop trail that follows Colter Bay shoreline with views of Jackson Lake and the Teton Range. Starting from the Colter Bay Visitor Center, the trail takes visitors through a forested area and along the shore of Jackson Lake. Lakeshore Trail is a great family friendly hike. Flat, easy, beautiful views of the mountains, and places to play in the lake or enjoy lunch.

Blacktail Ponds Overlook. Right off Highway 191 and 89 in Grand Teton National Park is Blacktail Butte Road that leads to the Blacktail Ponds Overlook. The paved parking area offers awesome views of the wildlife area with ponds, streams and the Grand Teton Mountain Range. Great place for the whole family to enjoy views of the park.

The Snake River Bridge has undergone construction, and it may look different now. It is located right off highway 189 near the town of moose. It is a very busy spot with many cars pulled off to the side of the road to take pictures. It offers awesome views of the river, the surrounding mountains and landscape. They say it is a great place to spot wildlife especially moose.

The Lupine Meadows Trailhead provides hikers the access to the heart of the Teton Mountain Range. To access this trail, you need to drive down the 1-mile Lupine Meadows dirt road off Teton Park Road. This 10-mile challenging hike passes by many mountain ranges, lakes and sightseeing spots. Wildlife is very common you may see deer, elk, moose, or even bear.

The Polecat Creek Loop is an easy 2.5-mile loop hike. Follow the trail as it travels through forests, meadows, and wetlands. This trail offers nature enthusiasts an opportunity to see the beauty of the park while keeping an eye out for the diverse array of birds and wildlife that live in the area. The Polecat Creek Loop is a great view of the park's serene landscapes, where every step reveals nature's undisturbed charm.

The Willow Flats Overlook offers excellent wildlife and scenic viewing opportunities. A great number of birds and mammals live in this area. The best viewing times are early morning and late evening. The view across Jackson Lake toward the Teton Mountain Range is stunning. This turnout is located off HWY 191 known as John D Rockefeller JR Parkway in the park.

Glacier View Turnout provides an awesome view of three Teton glaciers. Teton Glacier is the largest glacier in the park and is a remnant of the last ice age. Across the valley, the Tetons can be seen easily with no obstruction of your view. Glacier View Turnout is about 20 minutes north of the town of Jackson, WY, on US-191 N/US-26/US-89.

The Grand Teton Pathway is a bike path that extends from the town of Jackson, north to Antelope Flats Road. At Moose Junction the pathway follows the Teton Park Road to Jenny Lake The pathway follows the Teton Park Road. It is an excellent path for riding a bike. It is about 8 miles long and offers excellent views of the park.

Potholes Turnout. Looking past the Pothole Wayside sign toward a stand of conifer trees surrounded by sagebrush you will get a magnificent view of the mountain range. The potholes area was formed by large glaciers that eventually melted and left holes in the ground. This turnout is located along the Teton Park Road, along with many others.

Grand Teton

POTHOLES
TURNOUT

Fun Facts About Grand Teton

1. Grand Teton National Park is in northwestern Wyoming. At approximately 310,000 acres, the park includes the major peaks of the 40-mile-long Teton Range.
2. Grand Teton National Park is named for Grand Teton, the tallest mountain in the Teton Range. Grand Teton is the highest mountain at 13,775 feet high.
3. There are 134 named mountains in the Teton Range. The principal summits consist of several classic peaks referred to as the Cathedral Group.
4. Earthquakes gave rise to the 40-mile-long Teton Range, which sits on a fault line. Earthquakes caused blocks of land on both sides of the fault line to slip past each other. The west block rose upward to form the mountains while the east block dropped down to form the valley called Jackson Hole.
5. During the ice age, glaciers formed and sculpted the land. Ice up to 3,500 feet thick flowed across the valley floor and down the mountains, carving U-shaped canyons and jagged peaks like the Grand Teton.
6. Grand Teton National Park features 200 miles of hiking trails.

Things to Do and Places to Visit

Visitor Centers - Craig Thomas Discovery & Visitor Center. Laurance S. Rockefeller Preserve Center. Jenny Lake Visitor Center. Jenny Lake Ranger Station. Colter Bay Visitor Center. Flagg Ranch Information Station. National Elk Refuge & Greater Yellowstone Visitor Center.

Hiking. Explore hikes throughout Grand Teton National Park

Guided Tours & Hikes. Take a Guided Tour or Hike

Boating & Floating. Paddle on Jenny, String, Leigh, or Jackson Lake

Biking. Ride a Bike in Grand Teton.

Fishing. Fish for trout within valley and alpine lakes.

Climbing and Mountaineering. Climb in the Teton Range

Scenic Drives. Take a scenic drive for spectacular views.

Wildlife Viewing. See the wildlife in Grand Teton.

Bear and Wildlife Safety. Learn how to stay safe in bear country.

Camping. Find a place to camp in Grand Teton

Rangers. Attend a Ranger Led Program or Become a Junior Ranger

Author Page

Billy Grinslott & Kinsey Marie Books

Copyright, All Rights Reserved

ISBN – 9781965098004

Thanks

www.ingramcontent.com/pod-product-compliance
Lightning Source LLC
Chambersburg PA
CBHW060850270326
41934CB00002B/73